Published by Polari Press
polari.com @polaripress

ISBN: 978-1-914237-06-5

Printed by TJ Books using vegetable
inks on 80gsm paper. Typeset in
10/12 Roslindale.

Cover design and typesetting
by Peter Collins for Polari.

Edited by Amy Ridler.

This first edition was printed in
the UK in October 2023.

RISING OF THE BLACK SHEEP

LIVIA KOJO ALOUR

polari

IV. ANCESTRAL CALLINGS

V. THE RISE

This debut poetry collection is dedicated to all of my sisters out there in the diaspora, growing up & living without any knowledge of their heritage. Who, like me, are spending their lifetime looking for belonging, identity and love.

"If I didn't define myself for myself, I would be crunched
into other people's fantasies for me and eaten alive"
— Audre Lorde

"The one person who will never leave us, whom we will
never lose, is ourself. Learning to love our female selves
is where our search for love must begin"
— bell hooks

Introduction
Dr Marisa Carnesky

Livia Kojo Alour walked into one of my workshops in the early 2010s and I had no idea at that moment how central to my practice and to my life she would become. She was deeply respectful towards me and my teaching methods, she already had had exceptional skill as a performer, but she wanted more – she wanted to make challenging work and was open to experimentation in evolving her performance practice. She showed a feminist camaraderie and recognition that makes you feel like what you are doing it worth it. When you've been making live art and cabaret for thirty years on the margins, you can feel like the work you've done has been forgotten or unnoticed and it is rare and so affirming when an artist communicates respect and confidence in you. Feeling emboldened by her generosity, charm and positivity we set to work.

It started with Livia making a couple of new pieces, one burlesque that boldly explored what black face means to a woman of colour as a performer and unravelling notions of exotica. She also made a spoken word piece about her childhood, cleverly hinged around a Tina Turner song to comic effect. In both of these short pieces she was taking a risk with form and content that strayed significantly from established burlesque and club performances of the time. Here was she was talking, singing, questioning and challenging cultural identity and cultural appropriation in equal turn.

Her commanding stage presence was unquestionable and her physicality and skills showed a level of professional dance training and sophisticated movement awareness. Yet it was her writing and the originality of her concepts which was so exciting and engaging to watch unfolding in action. She was fearless to unwrap and explore taboos and try every performance form she could.

It was this extraordinary combination of writing and conceptual skills, stage presence, physical training and willingness to challenge and be challenged – to train further and take on new skills and ideas that made her stand out so significantly as an artist to watch – an artist with a vision that was clearly going to make an impact.

I see now that these performances already contained the seeds of her solo work *Black Sheep* and the extraordinary writing included in this book. Her poetry flows and in it you become immersed as an invited insider to a world that slips and shifts and negotiates through barriers, borders, risks, shifting identities, challenges, hustle, struggle, pain, triumph, queerness, showbiz strangeness and extraordinary endurance.

Her writing is both unwavering and precise in its observations of white privilege and living in a culture as a woman of colour where colonial patriarchal structures still govern our day to day lives. She finds herself in the arms of her white family trying so hard to raise their beautiful black daughter in the suburban white Germany of the 1980s and 90s, loving them yet realising her difference to them and the limits of emotional support when your child is continually othered. We discover the institutionalised racism she has lived through as a performing artist; having to address the clichés and the caretaking she is expected to take of her white peers as they carelessly address her with racist tropes and remarks, challenge her status and her equality. She fearlessly addresses the most difficult times, when industry 'professionals' expect her to make insulting compromises and take life threatening risks.

Yet throughout her poetic landscapes are dense and moving, she connects us emotionally to her experience whilst not excusing us for our part in the institutional racism and the voyeurism she has lived with all her life.

Working with Livia on the live show was a unique and fulfilling experience in dramaturgy – finding a visual devices from theatre and variety traditions that could illustrate and visually connect with her words as she moved through the stages of her performance. Seeing her commit and train over the last few years and evolve into a magnificent singer, taking on complex compositions and collaborating with other musicians to orchestrate her material and a wealth of interesting songs from across genres she has made her repertoire has been so exciting to see.

Audiences of *Black Sheep* are usually shocked – Livia's work is so deep and honest, and she is so in control of her material and so well-rehearsed, that they know immediately they are the grip of someone who commands and demands a growing international audience. Whilst you sit back and revel in her polished presence you are quickly jolted into the reality that this professionalism came with a price to her as an artist, as a woman and as a Showwoman. We watch her lifting herself, with all her power out of the margins and onto the world stage. A poet for our times that crosses between borders, between worlds and invites us to connect and explore otherness through her story and in ourselves. She is no longer the *Black Sheep* but an extraordinary new decolonising queer feminist voice, a new generation rewriting herstory.

If you can't bare
swimming this ocean of tears
walk against the tide

I

LETTERS FROM
THE UNDERDOG

The Beginning of All Times

Fat Freddy's Katze war dein lieblingscomic Benny Hill, The
Beatles, The Rolling Stones, der rock and roll verein/haarteile/
jade ohrringe/alles in grün immer wieder der absolut aller
letzte versuch/du hast den sarkasmus wirklich nicht
verstanden aber immer so getan/ketten rauchender
workaholic/die klassische übermutter mit dem lockeren
portmonee/wünsche gehen nur in erfüllung wenn womxn
bezahlt/geld oder religion/trotzdem wird in weiss geheiratet/
du konntest dich so derart unter den tisch trinken/am
nächsten morgen trotzdem leben retten engel in
weiss/radikal/trotzdem total
normal/überflieger/underrated/und wenn ich mich richtig
erinnere absolutely adorable

Oh mother, how i miss you

i walk down the lane
to my home for the last time
windy green leaves
floating ducks on a lake

where i grew up
time was always standing still
never seen the big city
from afar
idyllic heavenly & hell
bike rides early morning
a sweet pastry for lunch
wooden chairs
safe brick walls
of school times
but nothing
could prevent me
from getting hurt so deeply

Oh mother, how I miss you

a white beetle car
knackered from the '70s
a black and white cat in my crib
my grandmother
who used to be a nazi
hugging deeply
suffocating me
with their love

growing up wasn't easy
life ended early
society gaslit me out
i held onto optimism
only on the dance floor
full of synthetic love

Oh mother, how I miss you

i want to see the sun
shining wildly
though the leaves
have you ever had a forest
in your backyard?
mit blättern so grün
der erde so braun
moos überwachsenen steinen
gebrochene Äste
fallen trees

where your heart could sink
into a muddy footstep
on a rainy day
plucking worms
chasing beetles
feeding your imagination

i kneeled stealing milk
out of my cats feeding tray
flew to the moon
on a black table
kissed a girl, punched a boy
in primary school
nobody could stop me

i shaved my head
danced crying
for a lost future
in academia
rebelled until rebellion
became my identity
there is still no label that fits

Oh mother, how i miss you

you would have been so proud

i am everything

but conventional.

saw you die
open wounds that would never heal
there & then
i left you
i know what i have done
life has been hard
still
you are my angel
my guiding light

Oh mother, how i miss you

walking down memory lane
remember big trees

sunlight sparkling once more
i loved the big garden
the nature was freedom

wishing i could be a small child again
just for one day
come home from kindergarten
ripped open bleeding knees
sitting on the toilet seat
while you clean my wounds

feel the sting
of an alcohol wipe
hugs cries
for all our lost times

Oh mother, how i miss you

i'm happy you are gone
setting me free
to find my higher self

i have brothers and sisters now
fled white saviours

you have taught me
to be strong
i have always been much stronger

so
when the sun is shining
though the leaves
dripping
golden
memories
sparkling on my skin
I remember YOU
and my purpose
always

so very proud
of where I am from

Sweden

your holidays with my parents fishing
racing to catch a huge sword fish
ice cold dark glimmering lake under
stars moon & sun

sun swallows stars & moon
a yellow green grey sword fish
flapping for life

morning sky
eats clouds for breakfast
i am a bit cold
or feel sick
the fish already smells of death

you would have looked lovely
in jeans & t shirt

we don't like dad anymore
after killing a fish

Blue Like Denim

If teenage trauma was a fabric
it would be denim
high quality cotton
woven into indigo blue
as blue as my youth

when my whole inner circle
of porcelain   skinned   friends
grew into the perfect 501
I got stuck with the carrot jeans

felt like a farmer
between those thin giraffes
the media taught me
that was elegance
I   wasn't   a   classic
to be worn with cool tees

crying into cotton instead
for not being enough
because I wasn't fitting in
to the so desired blue jeans
the symbol
the proof
of my un-relatable
un-changeable

otherness

A Letter

Father
You haven't given me anything
when I needed it and so much less
I have wept at your feet
asking you to hit me
imagining this was the last strive to get any of your attention
You loved animals much more than human beings
even more than your own daughter
Was I your own daughter?

Our family lies were like tangled rope
sealed with speciality knots and never-ending loose ends
It was hard to make any sense of it
especially as a child

I understand now
that your sperm just wasn't fertile
This ripped a whole big piece
out of your confidence
so big you took a pact
with your mother
to blame your wife
saving you from the shame
as a strong German man
Your father could stay proud

It was an open lie
It drove us all insane

She adopted a black child
you had no say
I came home on her birthday
wrapped up
big shiny bow
A cute little gift

screaming kicking crying
A lonely little girl
she gave love
originally accounted for you

She had a place hidden in her heart
that was so big, warm & safe
A place you'd never found
cause you were drowning in self-pity
angry at the world
running from your parents' judgement blinded

I grew up
You grew only more attached to your lies
Hiding in our greenhouse

Counting fish

Researching plants

I turned 10
We didn't know each other
You'd never known your wife
She had a wonderful business
A thriving woman with everything
just in need of a lot more love
I was struggling
but since I was black
I was supposed to,
right?

You accepted we didn't need you
without even asking
if that was the truth

I watch you drink
fight with mum or just be gone

You only spoke to tell me to leave
You'd wear your dirty garden shoes
into our clean house

The only way to your attention
was shouting very loud
to break through to you
the result was only blame
Of course i turned aggressive
after watching you
ignoring me

Disturbing silence
A family made of few people
Not   just   one

I assured you I don't want you as my father
Started hating you
wished for a life just mother & me
Drew this out in beautiful daydreams
Planning our escape
for the day she'd leave you

Instead, she died

In this ill twist
We found us standing back to back
You, me, 17 years later
Fearful of an unknown future
Grieving the soul that brought us together

I still denied to receive your hate
You finally exploded
hit me
We would never heal together

Father you have long been gone too
I've never dared to speak this way
must admit
I do a lot of things the way you did
inherited the way how you loved to be alone

As much as I wanted to hate you
I love you, I miss you

So sorry for the things that are beyond our control

Oh So Other

Oh so other
19 76 15 35
A nobody
like everyone expected me to be
I want to be somebody
stand out
make a difference
prove I was worth the bother

Oh so other
19 76 15 40
Tired
of being brushed under the carpet
Hungry to change the world
to transform into a warrior queen
My picture on a billboard
over highways in dual realities
counting shiny bills
stuffing them into the bedlinen
being *somebody* feels so different

from what I expected it to feel

Oh so other
19 76 15 16
I am frighting with swords now
against the eyes of the boy
who rejected me because
I looked more Mad Max than Whitney Huston
because singing sexy to a man
was as alien to me as I was alien to them
Naturally took male dancers as my influence
MTV flickering in the background
who would have known
I'd be a femme and boi one day

Stomping the patriarchy naked
while smoking an imaginary cigarette

Oh so other
19 76 15 20 10
For every man
that me eyed up and down
Disgusting lust perpetuating harmful stereotypes
For every door
that was pushed into my face
declaring me not worthy
of entering a sacred white space
for every time getting paid less
being called names

stupid
ugly
old
lazy
bitch
too much too little

Ohh so other
19 76 15 20 15
Multi-disciplinary performance art
weakness for outlandish glamour
Tragically beautiful
glorious, just astonishing
Stop stabbing yourself
senseless
moulding metal blades
hot from anger
Maybe I wasn't made for this
is anybody?
I don't appreciate
the lived through trauma
to find myself
on top as a black performer

Oh so other
19 76 15 20 19
I'm not angry
I'm tired & angry
Fuck you institutional racism
I've decolonised myself
moving forward without you

Oh so other
19 76 15 2020
Walking as a black example of excellence
role model, mother to many black children
door opener, stage heroine, warrior queen
I've transcended the stereotypes
proudly let the good African hair
float around my cheek bones
like a phoenix risen from the ashes
reversed internalised racism
created joy out of pain
I want to give this present to the world
humble, vulnerable
honest & kind
but I understand
not everyone will listen to the Black woman

We. Are. Other.

The Single Black Curl

At the dinner party a white woman takes a packet of
weave-on hair out of her handbag while shaking her head
with laughter. The blonde ponytail whipping around her
face

I think to myself
you don't have to be afraid

She says: Look at this piece of cheap synthetic! My
Husband brought it from the dollar shop it's a present for
me. Just for a laugh. We do that sometimes.

Do what? Exchange microaggressions into blatant racism
in front of a black person
for fun?

Why are you so mad? It's just a single black curl!
A device that threatens the world
A gunshot killing without regret
A terrorist with all the power

The white woman's going on and on about the weave. She
says: With this price tag (Now waving it directly into my
face). It looks so cheap we gonna appropriate the living
hell out of it!
As much as we like
for as long as want
Throw it into the circus
make it twirl
like a minstrel

Then I'll stick it onto your head making you the big
showdown of the night just watch...

We'll give you hell if you don't obey or dig your grave if
you keep wearing it out
you keep wearing it out
you keep wearing it out

Stop! You're wearing me out

She says: You don't have to be afraid! it's just for a laugh!

Meanwhile the single black curl is doing a twirl in its
plastic bag. The Woman was laughing when she put the
bag onto the table. The bag with my hair. With that single
black curl. The pubic hair that doesn't grow in between
white women's legs

We will oppress you
We will possess you
We will betray you
We will break you
We will straighten you

Then we'll put you into this plastic bag and bring you back
to the shop.
So we can get our money back!
Because you are worthless!

I heard how she laughed with the bag in her hand.
My heart just melted.

Evil Power
Evil Black Power
Evil Woman
Evil Black Woman
Evil Witch
Evil Black Witch
Evil Black Witch Woman
With pubic hair on her head

Now the white woman laughs in anger throwing her head
back so possessed and enraged of a single black curl.
That's coming from the shop just to entertain her. That's
going back to the shop because it wasn't worth her while. I
wasn't worth her while.
Why the fuss?
How can hair be so threatening?
What has she got to lose?

Nothing. But her privilege.
She needs to keep that at a 1,000%

II

STAND UP &
RAISE A FIST

I am a Black woman and I'd lie to say I am not angry.
But nobody has the right to define me solely through this.
Nobody has the right to deny me my anger.
Nobody has the right to judge me by my anger.
Try to embrace being uncomfortable in the next chapter.
Remember at least, you can choose when to read it.

yesterday

deep maim
great wounds
paper knife pain

perforated
holding you
exchange me
for more suffering

moments of
intimate abuse
insist on narcissistic
personality traits

forgiven mistakes
used me too
love conditionally

believed
i was nothing
without you

dependency
your oxygen
chasing daily hits

torn apart
let me live for
another tomorrow

but at next tomorrow's dawn
i finally stood up
to dance
til soul's sunset

picked a knife
cut your ties
out of my brain

yesterday
will always remember
an insurance policy
for tomorrow

Double Standards

vulnerability
evil listens
shine a light there

something in society
clings on the shamed female stereotype
to subdue her strength

are men wild and exciting?
womxn are weak
everyone is watching
call her a whore

the humxn mind is so conditioned
deep inside of us
the truth lingers
all benefit

misogyny's roots
big branches
all are part of the problem
surreptitiously feel safety
in double standards.

slut shaming
rape culture
bullying
harassment
the other way looking
victim blaming
racism

find your strength
to speak up
against oppression

work these streets
dismantle internalised beliefs
how about you?

Are you Mulatto?

Performance piece with drum

You are so special *(Drum)*

You are so beautiful *(Drum)*

You are so special so so special

What are you? *(Drum)*

> Are you Mulatto? *(Drum)*
> Are you Mulatto? *(Drum)* Are you Mulatto?
> Mulatto Macchiato?

You don't seem so aggressive *(Drum)*

But you are a little too ambitious *(Drum)*

I am so so sorry
I am so so sorry
I am so sorry for your hair

It must be so horrible to have hair like this!
I am so sorry so so sorry

It's nice to be around you *(Drum)*

But you are a little too ambitious *(Drum)*

What are you? *(Drum)*

> Are you Mulatto? *(Drum)*
> Are you Mulatto? *(Drum)* Are you Mulatto?
> Mulatto Macchiato?

Or something like that?

You know... like mixed or mixed race or something like that?

Because you are so beautiful *(Drum)*
But a little too ambitious *(Drum)*

Ride me really wild. Fuck me really hard. Ride me really
wild and speak dirty German to me *(Drum)*
Don't be so over sensitive *(Drum)*
Just ride me really hard and speak some dirty German to me
You can't be my girlfriend
No reason really, I just don't feel it that way with you *(Drum)*
I mean come on you know…You know what I mean? *(Drum)*

Do you know what I mean? *(Drum)*

What are you? *(Drum)*

Are you Mulatto? *(Drum)*
Are you Mulatto? *(Drum)* Are you Mulatto?
Mulatto Macchiato?

You know what I mean?

Like mixed race?
Like is your dad black or white or what are you?

Are you a witch? *(Drum)*

You can't be my girlfriend!

No reason really, I just don't feel it that way with you *(Drum)*

But your skin   Is   So   Soft
It's So soft *(Drum)*
So soft *(Drum)*
So soft *(Drum)*
So soft *(Drum)*
So soft *(Drum)*
So soft *(Drum)*
So soft *(Drum)*
So soft *(Drum)*

What are you? *(Drum)*

Are you Mulatto? *(Drum)*
Are you Mulatto? *(Drum)* Are you Mulatto?
Mulatto Macchiato?

You know what I mean?
I don't see colour!
I am a good person!
I don't see colour!
I've never seen any colour but i need to know
what you are!

You speak dirty German, but you look like this
What the fuck are you? *(Drums wildly for a few seconds)*

I am Black.

My Anger

My anger
a nasty outpour of acid
raining on my skin
far too vital
burning sensations of violence

My anger
an endless list of stuffed feelings
crawling out of the bedsheets
grief i've been carrying
mixed with other people's opinions

My anger
stifles me
since the fucking end of times

My anger
keeps looking
into the same old face
what brought us here
is what keeps us here

My anger
keeps me on low reserves
unescapable pain
wherever i put my feet

My anger
has no home
but lives on
to feed my art

My anger
overpriced excess baggage
carry on to interpersonal disputes

My anger
reaching through my bedroom door
i'd rather work forever
than let it sleep next to me

My anger
fighting my own black & white

My anger
wants to be just black

My anger
a display of today's feelings
tomorrow's feelings

My anger
a force within
always drawing outwards to explode

My anger
until we find a way out
it stays with me

My anger
whispers
be more furious
never   be   free

Riot Poem

If you'd ask / I don't want to teach you / but you don't ask
so there is no solution that pleases both & I am already
beyond caring

My heart is so broken with 1,000 pieces lying over floor
all I do is kneeling
without dustpan
or brush
picking up the pieces of a life that I didn't even want in the
first place

How can I be fulfilled without a counter part?
you make my suffers real
while I am listening to your demanding voice
calling me / asking me / pinning questions for more
& more

In my wildest dreams I could tell you to stop

My body felt so worthless I fled my own existence just to
be freed from the patriarchal abusive racist system laid
upon generations of Black womxn

A strong back means nothing if you don't have the will
to make it move

As long as we can walk / we can walk out
As long as we can run / we can run away

But today I recommend to go out into the streets to march
& protest the inequality of our Black lives and shout:

We were never made to be tortured
Therefore, are still owed reparations for 500 years of pain

Understand that the now changing landscape / statue by
statue / are only symbolistic giveaways
that. repair. nothing.

more has to be done

Protest against the continuous exploitation of our
coolness, our swag, our intelligence, our workforce.
We Black people are no more to be killed / erased /
recycled / or made god like

We are humxn in our humxn right

When I look at your hands
your soft touch is far from perfect
In your sparkling immaculate nails I only see white
supremacy
dripping like an acidic nail varnish onto the fragile skin of
your Vietnamese nail technician

Your hands have never cleaned an attic full of oppressed
ancestry
Your hands where never soaked in blood of your own
history / written on lies and pain that recurs as trauma
through generations and generations

Your hands never washed a newborn baby believing it was
already dead just because of the colour of its skin

Your hands are so sensitive they only portray white
fragility
Their softness is an insult to each and every cocoa
buttered nation of the African continent

I am drained from overthinking
how I can heal or even breathe
It's impossible to erase the memory of my own kind being
killed in the streets for

no. other. reason.
but hate.

For weeks month & years I have done nothing else than
work on a better future for the next generation
Yet you will be awarded a prize for the good work
you didn't do

Looking at this reality
I get often lost in time because the pain & shaming has
been endless for hundreds of years

What am I fighting for if nobody will ever respect me for
who I am
Yet it is hope that makes me strong again
That rebuilds my muscles every time I fall apart making
my whole existence an artwork of resilience endlessly
exhibited into your daily life
When will you notice?

Can we make life a matter of change that lets us live
equally ever after?

Can we stop living the white lies of history and
acknowledge the wrongdoing of your ancestors?

Can we stop police brutality
systemic racism
and modern slavery
or is this just another episode of

Where   is   the   lie?

White Tear

I see a white tear
rolling down a cheek
move in closer
ohhh white tear
the only pain I enjoy
let it roll
burn the skin
wade in the water
when its drips softly
out of that eye
she said
it's so hard to be white
that's why I write

White tear
standing in your privilege
have you ever felt the pain
of being ostracised?
because your hair grows up not down
your skin never mirrors current beauty standards
you're just not represented in the media
or if you are
as a dead body shot

White tear
with astounding confidence
you walk into any space
like it was created just for you
you use my people as comforters
as if they were only born for you

You
got the audacity
to cry unasked on my shoulder about
how unfair the world is treating you

expecting me to understand your pain
in the rare incidence your privilege is failing

dare to speak to me like we are equal
only if you need something
asking me to wipe your tears
then send you back on your way
oppressing me

I see a white tear
dripping out of that eye
wade in that water
she said
it's so hard to be white
that's why I write

Brother
how internalised is your racism?
do you realise
you centre around white people
defend their every word
take from us to make space for them
choose to marry white
to opt for light skin privilege
for your children
instead creating dark skin privilege
to set things right

how does it feel to wake up
next to the proclaimed normal
is it really such a buzz?
liberating to never go back to black?
do you feel more comfortable?
I want to know
if love really doesn't see colour
because if humxns don't
we get so mad

Brother
do you comfort her
when she suffers consequences of her whiteness
when she goes through tough times
being denied something insignificant
when her ignorance triggers you

I see a white tear
rolling down a cheek
I move in closer
wade in the water
wade in the water children
wade in the water
she said
it's so hard to be white
that's why I write

White tear
i remember you
judging me
for having all these curves
who'd would have known you
always wanted to be black
how does it feel to be the status quo?
still wanting that ass
how does it feel to appropriate my figure
and oppress the culture that comes with it?

don't you think it's strange
you want to look like me
be like me
yet force your black partner
to look the other way
when you're passing on the street?
can you sleep at night
have you grown a conscience yet?

                    I see a white tear
                 when its drips softly
                    out of the eye
                  wade in the water
                      she said
                it's so hard to be white
                  that's why I write

Sister
do you think you parents rather accept
you if she's white?
how much do you hate yourself?
it's too radical to self-love
or embrace being other

can you soothe your identity crisis
with proximity to whiteness
do you feel less brown?
erasing the traits
that make you so beautifully different

does it comfort you
to live with someone who
hasn't experienced our pain and
deep sitting racial trauma?

                        I see a white tear
                     rolling down a cheek

and I ponder on reasons
why we can't move forward

are our people
too busy comforting white tears?
instead of
crying their own
drying their own
loving their own

I see a white tear
rolling down a cheek
I move in closer
wade in the water
ohhh white tear
the only pain I enjoy
let it roll
burn the skin

Cut-Throat

*In 2021, 14% of the UK population identified as Black,
Asian & global majority with London having over 40% of
its population identifying as such. Many of their ancestors
migrated from ex-colonial countries making London one of
the most ethnically diverse cities in the world.*

—

The 2020 report
of the Commission on Race and Ethnic Disparities
detected no institutional racism in Britain

inequality can't be linked to social class **cut-throat**
discrimination detector unavailable **cut-throat**
we don't live in a post-racial society **cut-throat**

keep calm – carry on
keep watching TV
protest against murders
outside of your country

I can't breathe

there is nothing to breathe in here
breathing is overrated

ethnic minorities
outperforming their white peers **cut-throat**

                    still forced to take
            offered minority scholarships **cut-throat**

sponsored oppressed skin colour
produces a main income **cut-throat**

picked up as a pick me
picking away on the soft coloured skin **cut-throat**

expected to be the cleaner
literally metaphorically **cut-throat**

uphold the system
perpetuating our own oppression **cut-throat**

there is no pride in a label
that was never fit for human definition **cut-throat**

you can talk but not too loud
you can play but you can't win
you can live but don't live big
you can be but don't take up space

let me murder your expectation
question prejudice
deconstruct the social ranking system
cut-throat
cutting up society
my words become swords
this one is hard to swallow

you can
i could
just be careful
it doesn't

cut your **throat**

III

BLACK QUEER LOVE

Ode To My Queerness

8
I once kissed a girl
It unleashed a strange word less
desire tingling down my spinal cord
estranging me from
the too small heteronormative quiet room
I was pushed in at birth
to reduce the amount of stimulation
keeping me safe from possibilities

7
Trying too hard to fit in
desperate attempts, hiding the shame
of not being asked to the dance

being the only girl having to hold onto her father's arm
instead of her boyfriends

dancing humiliation away on a ball
only to trip over
what was planned as a seamless transition
falls apart into a seamstress ambition
in form of my grandmother fixing a gown right there
on the dance floor

6
The girls stopping me before school
checking my fingernails
laughing about my obvious fail
to paint them red in an elegant manner
the dried nail varnish on my unruly cuticles
perfectly presents my feelings towards femininity

5
holding hands with the neighbours boy
women   sex   power   ghetto blaster
urban fantasies,
fetishisation of the black womxn
labelled heartbreak when he
walked away with my white friend

      being marriage material is a concept of oppression

I was a thing people would wear with their new hoodie
cause I looked cool

4
The strange world of gay boys in the '90s
was the nearest I got to experiencing liberation
a side kick to flash about
but leave standing at the entrance of the darkroom
the flashing mirror verse disco ball
had me in tears when no one hugged me
coming up on E

3
I slept with the girlfriend
               of the boy I thought I fancied

She touched me quickly in unknown ways

    extracted my soul from the poetry I wrote about lovers

only to drop it into a cold ocean
of fear

2
I don't love myself enough
to acknowledge suffering
hunting desire only to be hurt
Debating internal change
amid my world coming to pieces
I hold my breath & dive
taking strides to ice cold waters
surpassing the north peak of emotions
frozen eyes in flight can't blink

1
I rise up
out of the ocean

0
Once I swam the ocean of fear
Walked against the tide of pain
Laid on a hot bed of nails
like it was a beach
Cached & swallowed
the flaming sword falling from heaven
My desires became my normality
The patriarchal, colonial
can't pressure me anymore
No more feeling of undeserving
could ever weigh heavy enough
to dissolve the scars of my struggle
Pain connected my dots
& set me free

Heteronormative

a dirty nightclub
with the girl on the dance floor
we touched wet lips

loud music pumping
feet stomping to the rave beat
Berlin at its best

ripping my net top
she whispered come with me
in 1990

something beautiful
rips my heart open
unforgettable

impossible to
know it will be decades till
I make it my truth

curiosity
a forbidden taste like straight
heteronormative lesbian porn

try un-feel feelings
never considered her through
this conditioned gaze

you finally ignite
dim irrational feelings
for the after taste

this strong taste a clear
testament on how much I
hated pussy right?

conveniently
I suffered 10 more long years
on my assumption

societies norm
there was something wrong with me
I believed it

successful dancer
easy for the trap money
striptease's hard sell

keeping a busy head
world travelling to stay single
self-destructive mind

but now I allow
myself to truly feel again
to desire a need

aged in these dark times
there was she to bring light
and all was clear now

how I missed this huge
detail so long truly doesn't
matter anymore

verlorene liebe

guten morgen vergangenheit
versuche nicht mit mir zu flirten
deine sonne geht auf
und mein herz fällt herunter
es war richtig dich zu verlassen

a love lost

good morning my ex-lover
don't you ever try flirt with me again
when your sun rises
my heart always sets
the best decision was to leave for good

BLACK LOVE

~~white love~~ BLACK LOVE

~~white love~~ doesn't
BLACK LOVE is unpacking stereotypes under the
christmas tree

~~white love feels~~
BLACK LOVE is fire

~~white love~~ BLACK LOVE is a rainbow ~~without its colours~~
BLACK LOVE births rainbows

~~white love~~ BLACK LOVE will ~~whip up a storm~~
BLACK LOVE is the calm after the storm

~~white love~~ has your blackness on display 24/7
BLACK LOVE protects you

~~white love keeps you fragile on a daily tightrope walk~~
BLACK LOVE is the whole ~~fucking~~ circus

~~white love~~ might lose you
BLACK LOVE is finding yourself

~~white love~~ needs an apology to exist
BLACK LOVE is unapologetic

~~white love wants to be~~ romantic
BLACK LOVE is romance

~~white love is~~ writing history
BLACK LOVE is re-writing history

~~white love~~ listens to ~~Elvis~~ stolen music
BLACK LOVE is Jazz, Blues, Rock, Electronic...

~~white love is maybe~~ beautiful & dramatic
BLACK LOVE touches your soul

~~white love for one last time~~
BLACK LOVE forever

I Quit Love

Surreptitiously, I quit love

because I've believed for too long that love wasn't made for me. Decades of hope shattered by failure to ignite my heart the way literature speaks of love.

The romantic dream, poets describe like walking heaven on earth.

It scares me.

It feels like an ephemeral cavalcade of happiness that always ends in subjugation. It feels like riding a Russian roulette rollercoaster with a broken carriage waiting.

I feel jealousy

towards everyone who claims they've experienced real love while I am struggling to decide if it really exists.
The uncertainty is jarring.
The suspension is injurious. I don't want to expose myself to these feelings anymore. Always looking from the outside in.
Never allowing myself to partake.

That's why I am quitting love today.

To free myself from expectation.
To be a clean slate.
To stop the waiting.
The pain of disappointment.
To just go about my life.
To build myself up strong.
To learn how to love myself first.
To strip myself strategically from past trauma.

To be ready to let life beautifully surprise me when I am
not expecting it.

Surreptitiously I am quitting love today
only to be ready for it when it's finally my turn.

Love Is Controversial

I'm falling in love

terrified
impossible
to rely on the work I've done on myself
not hurt you
not to hurt us
love is blinding
love is binding
love is controversial

your love

petrifies me
to be too drunk in love
to fall into a bottomless mimosa
to be too tipsy
fall over onto my face
hurt my skin
break a tooth
or my heart
love is controversial

we say we fall

I don't want to hit rock bottom
why don't we fly in love
take off like beautiful birds
revolving around each other in the air
no
we fall in love descending
is there love underground?
love is controversial

romanticising something

we are so hesitant of
giving up autonomy
sharing our deepest feelings thoughts and secrets
aren't they made to be kept
from each other?
from another?
love is controversial

we intentionally disclose information
that was intended to stay hidden
so carefully from the world
for a lifetime

practice vulnerability
exercise sensibility
execute radical tenderness
risk our safety
open up the doors of our personal haven
share responsibility
with no idea if it's worth it
if it pays back
if the reward is
elated shared compromise in unity

love is controversial

oh boi
do I love a good controversy

IV

ANCESTRAL CALLINGS

Travelling

I remember sitting on the typewriter
writing my personal songs of sorrows when only 17
A typewriter from the sixties grey battered secretary style
I often wonder where this old typewriter went when I left
home to travel the world to collect stories

I walked uphill without shoes Carrying my heart around
the universe from one side to the other
I picked a star Burned my soft hand I loved the moon Rode
on the milky way Caressed the sunset Swam in every
ocean Danced with the starfish Heard whales cry Crossed
every desert Died 100 deaths under their green glowing
nights while hearing bombs fall
I bought a camel only to set it free Took the Orient Express
Admired heavy snowfall Caught a polar bear fed him fish
Stole an iceberg in heart shape Crossed Greenland by foot
I switched on the Northern Lights
Twice
I touched every skyscraper Flew on a falcon Slept on
cloud I got lost in a swamp wading through knee-deep
waters Played the saxophone in a street parade Climbed
every ancient pyramid to sacrifice birds Made love to
many strangers Got arrested into a dark cold jail Time
travelled to pre-colonial times I learn about my ancestor's
spirituality Then met my mother Birthed children Created
magic spells
I learned how to swallow swords but failed to rewrite
history
Now I am sitting at a 100 year old wooden writing desk
about to pick up a pen to write down my stories.
They are so complex
Cluttering my thoughts
If I remember all the details – what will happen to me after
I've written them down?

Black Womxn

Black Womxn
Goddesses
Earth Mothers
Queens

Black womxn
cherish a simple moment
but burn at everyone's despise

Black womxn
never get a break
expected to be warriors
teachers
cleaners
nannies
best friends
not lovers

Black womxn
go unnoticed
do they really exist?

Black womxn
stand up straight
smiling proud while beaten
radiating a love they have never been allowed
to experience
themselves

Black Womxn
Goddesses
Earth Mothers
Queens

Black womxn
the roots of
our erasure
stripped naked
folded blind
fed to our own kind
they have eaten to survive

Black womxn
worked
laughed through pain
silenced by torture
weeped without a sound
Black womxn
survived

Black womxn
our ancestors
stars have not been burned
still shining bright

Black Womxn
Goddesses
Earth Mothers
Queens

Persevere

Auction

Next up

one Black femxle
getting trap money
on the entertainment industry's
auction block
I grew up being afraid of dogs

wade in the water
no house I ever lived in felt safe
wade in the water
I once let a white man whip me
in a fetish club
wade in the water
pain & misery
on the run for too long
wade in the water
over 3 million Africans
were bought by Britain
wade in the water
we forget
London was a major centre
of the slave trade
I live here now
wade in the water

we've exchanged colonialism
against capitalism
trap money
strange fruit
I can't be sold
where do I go back to

Bow Down

A date once
called me a narcissist
judging the pictures
on my wall
she long gone

love yourself
proud
be a celebration
it's your life
your terms

coffee brown skin
carries DNA
of everything
survival instincts
survived within

gut feelings
meditation
hunting reason
ceremonial beginnings
celestial cleansing

rituals

throw me a daily struggle

my mission
not a victim
report Black
to the ancestors
with art

prevail
fight harder
repair the past

walk into the future
smiling

look young
while getting old
every lynched brother
had a sister
with eternal beauty

fuel
feed me hurdles
knock them
spikes in running shoes
lost against a white girl
sometimes
internalised stereotypes
burn my eyes

cancelled
fingerprints
I will not stop existing
uncomfortable
ignorant
colonial snobbery

wake up

still beautiful
Black goddesses
crowns with postcodes
legs to die for
skin as canvas

communicate
with Black angels
Afro futuristic queen
re-incarnated slaves

I am proud
be proud

scrying mirror

she woke up one morning
screaming
the past had called
her soul travelled
several thousands of years
through hot deserts
cold streams
of the motherland

she embodied children
preparing to birth through mothers
held hands with the dying
while walking them over

she stole thoughts of priests
harvesting information
we needed to survive

she danced in steamy rituals
channelling goddesses' glory
painting faces
with menstrual blood
laying naked
embracing burning skies
ready to conceive

dusty meltdowns
under crying trees
whispering secrets
into air vaults of time
filled with love
for our ancestors' future
circling around the planet
chased by death

eye to eye
she had no fears
when the dark lion
finally presented itself

she walked into his open mouth
with anticipation
spiritual rebirth
lets her live & die fearless

she is the messenger
she can't be killed

We Know the Way

Our ancestors knew the way
follow your inherited inner voice
  though the deserts
  through the forests
  thought the waters
  through the rain
every tribe has a place
beyond our collective pain
to get back to

Over all the continents
we are the children of our land
deep in our conscious souls

                we know where we belong

The truth lies protected
past stories recalled in dreams
listen to the spirits
who are hiding in our gut
they will guide us
  though the deserts
  through the forests
  thought the waters
  through the rain
finally to show us the place
beyond our collective pain

                we can get back to

V

THE RISE

Dear White People

Dear white people
I'm done saying thank you for letting me stand on your
table. I am claiming the table. This bloody old wooden
monolith you have sat on for 500 years needs to be burned
in a huge fire. We've got some decolonising to do.

Dear white people
There is no reason for you to be upset tired or confused.
There is no space left for white fragility. You need to Black
woman up and fight

Dear white people
We owe you nothing. No smile no nice gesture no
explanation. If you by now don't know what's up you truly
don't deserve to know. Just go back to your yoga class, golf
course, play station or law firm & shut the fuck up.

Dear white people
If you feel woke let me tell you you are not. Stop claiming
terms to make them yours. Stop gentrifying the Black
Lives Matter movement for the sake of bandwagon
culture. We see all of it. Being tired is not a comprehensive
enough term anymore to describe our feelings.

Dear white people in show business
Don't wait for us to come onto your Instagram to correct
the mistakes you made while sharing our pictures.
Your counterproductive arrogant artificial support is
insensitive and insulting.

Dear white people all around the world
We kinda don't need you anymore. We are the new
producers,   curators,   owners   & employers.
Get used to the feeling of being left standing outside in the
rain. No servant with an umbrella will come save you this
time.

Dear white people
Stop explaining to us our world. You just have such big
mouth because colonialism is your great-grandmother.
With her passing your privilege was passing too. You keep
overstaying your welcome. You keep interfering with our
future. We won't let this happen anymore.
You will stand in front of the grand jury. A room full of
Black judges. You will answer every question, apologise
& pay back reparations for as many years as slavery and
colonialism lasted.

Dear white people
You   are   guilty   until   proven   innocent.

External Colours

On this palatable colour of skin
I wonder the two worlds
worship my mixed heritage
from pale to golden brown glowing

My parents were white

                              who am I to dismiss?

They've adopted me
nurtured me
kicked my ass

Perfection is flaw
you can love & dismay
the same situation
It's your power not a weakness

My father was an animal man
he nurtured creatures / critters / plants
& German beer

My mother was a healer
who worked too hard
died while helping others

Good people come in many colours
most white re-incarnated from the Black
lies or truth
there is no doubt
we need to look into that mirror

Now I am the animal man & healer
Before healing there is so much pain
Feelings are granted collective
only that one could run
the other one can't

Take to a mirror
Seek your salvation

The image behind it
tells you who you really are

Becoming the healer
is nothing short of internal
no matter what your external colours are

A Solution

Don't call me mulatto
mulatto it is a derogatory word
It derives from the term for 'young mule'
I am not a hybrid
I am not mix of horse & donkey
It's just lazy to carry on colonial traditions
We are way beyond using slavery's terms
Make the effort & let it look effortless

I am no mulatto.

Don' t call me German
I was born into a country that had no place for me
A government that played white saviour
That forced my mom to give me up
& that's still
46 years later
constantly asking for gratefulness for letting me live
breathe
eat
work
& pay taxes

I am no German.

Don't call me Black
Black is a constructed concept to continue segregation
Black prevents you from actually learning anything
about me
Black is a political standpoint
As an identity it erases culture
Black may describe the African American experience
but at the price of excluding the melanin of the rest of
the world Ask a proud African if they would give up their
amazing heritage for being Black

Black is a simplification for all the shades of Brown Don't
just call me Black

I am not only Black

Don't call me half white
Because this is a non-concept
My blood is red
my organs are red
my soft tissue is yes red
My thinking is conditioned by institutionalised racism
My actions are forced to manoeuvre around white privilege
You calling me half white
feels like my cup is half empty or
I don't have enough Black power shining through my light
You're calling me half white implies that my lighter shade
of brown is more accommodating for your gaze & less
threatening to your existence
I am not here to please you
Don't be fooled by my appearance

I am everything but half white

Don't call me coco
Chocolate Honey Brown Sugar
Coffee Caramel Latte Macchiato
Fetishise my dark skin & character?
Minimise me to a commodity? No!
Complimenting Black people by comparing them to food
is derogatory
Highlighting your kinky craving on our back is
dehumanising Cocoa and coffee are directly linked to
slavery With eating us you want to perpetuate your
position of power?
If your dark fantasy is becoming a slave master
you're 500 years late
Don't call me coco

I am not your slave

Don't ever call me nigger
In my school we had a game
Who is afraid of the nigger
The kid who plays the nigger had to chase the others &
catch them
We were taught that in sports
The nigger was the dangerous man
I grew up afraid of Black men because they were niggers
We had a sweet sold in our shops called nigger kisses
You go to the shop to buy a nigger kiss for less than 25p
A nigger kiss is worthless
Being referred to as dangerous & cheap are
my personal experiences with the word nigger
I don't want to reclaim the word

So don't you ever call me Nigger

I'll give you a solution to stop the constant fight.
How about you call me humxn
& respect my humxn right.

Nobody like us

Nobody like us

like water
like salt
like sugar
like red wine
dry but fruity
sweet & fly

Nobody like us

sparkling skin
happy
glowing
beautiful queens

Nobody like us

underwater
mystery
of the deep sea
deep feelings
popping ears
offloading pressure

Nobody like us

soft velvet
paws like a kitten
viciously scratching
carefully caressing
purring
loving
hungry

Nobody like us

always sad & happy
paranoid but calm
anxiously humming a soothing song
liberated within patriarchy
free but never satisfied

Nobody like us

floating
out of space
moon walking
stepping on stones
clearing the view
into the future
inviting you to look

Nobody like us

unlikely
to be like you
but liking you
unconditionally
true & truthfully
fully embodying
the body of time
around us

Nobody like us

special
don't let us walk away
let us walk in
instead

Nobody like us

your chance
to dance
to experience
transcendence
a piece of us
spiritually
emotionally
freely

Nobody like us

Overcoming

every individual human story
can teach us something
subliminal
or consciously
if we only pay attention

from these stories
i've learned
that our bodies carry
divine healing power within

unconnected

to religious orientation

I sat with Christians
sat with Hindi
sat with Tamil
sat with Muslim
and Buddhists

listened to their stories
of overcoming
pain, fear & great loss

read between their lines
of hope forgiveness & regrets

sailed along
thought their personal oceans of tears

held their hearts
in my hand
feeling their heartbeat

borrowed their souls
for trips with the Bennu Bird
through the underworld
back into the light

I let them tattoo
their darkest memories
ritualistic onto my skin

we climbed mountains together
to read our future
from the clouds

drank rejuvenation waters
from the secret springs
in lost forests

dug deep holes
into the ground
to hide & recharge
before facing our fears again

returning from these
intentionally deep
humxn exchanges
I brought a catalogue of thought

studying the healing
for over 1,000 years
the answers are
individually complex

we all carry
divine healing within us
whatever our land
whatever our believes

tapping into the ancient spirits
directing their love
towards ourselves
will guide us
out of misery
into understanding
how to move within the light

i've seen it
now think on it
every day

overcoming
a process we go through
from birth to death
subliminal
or consciously
if we only
pay attention

reflecting

walking the forest
beneath the surface linger
powerful pieces

detaching motion
my body floats around me
melting head to toe

envisioning the
puzzle complete piece by piece
solved framed past preset

I dream my future
continuously arranging
the floating pieces

centring around
my internal universe
subconscious collides

in the dark forest
dancing to the sound of owls
with my naked feet

on moist moss sinking
footsteps the present dissolves
momentarily

meditation time
gratefulness to be alive
I see the pictures

forming right in front
my hands holding their frames tight

I am complete now

Good Hair

The past:

bonnets are ghetto
wigs are hiding something underneath
braids are acceptable
natural hair is not

Me:

ode to you my friend
curly twisted zigzag bent
feisty spiralling out of my head
with bossy captivating 3 4 abc
wet or dry
always 100 percent curly
death defying gravity ignoring
connection to my ancestors
textured truth of the African diaspora
coarse rebellient
like a prayer growing up
a little dry sometimes
like a good wine
your glow shines through the ancient books
connects me to my Afro future

velvet
spongy
shea butter coated delight

nappy
platted
curled very tight

braided
textured
longing for more

I love you
my afro-textured hair

ode to you my friend
curly twisted zack zack bent

My Body Is...

My body is not
To be fetishised

My body is not
Too much

My body is not
Aggressive

My body is not
To be judged

My body is not
A costume

My body is not
A disability

My body is not
A dartboard

My body is not
A commodity

My body is not
A playground for injustice

My body is
Human

My body is
Sensitive

My body is
Political

My body is
Unpolitical

My body is
A sex symbol
when I wanted it to be

My body is
Asking for respect

My body is
Beautiful

My body is
Radically tender

My body is
Powerful

My body is
Free

My body is Black

Notes

'The Beginning of All Times' is dedicated to my beloved late mother

'Yesterday' is for every womxn who has survived an abusive relationship

'Riot Poem' is dedicated to George Floyd

'Cut-Throat' was inspired The 2020 U.K. report of the Commission on Race and Ethnic Disparities and written shortly after the Euro coup finals. It's dedicated to the three Black Black Footballers who missed their penalty shots and endured racial abuse after: Marcus Rashford, Jadon Sancho and Bukayo Saka

'We know the way' was inspired by the movie *Black Panther*. From the scene flying for the first time into Wakanda

'Good Hair' is dedicated to my afro and the seven years it took me to grow and learn how to love it

'My Body Is...' is dedicated to my friend and mentor Guillermo Gómez-Peña

Acknowledgements

I have deep love for my parents who, while alive, did everything in their power to help me become a successful strong womxn that can fiercely believe in herself and who, beyond their passing, are still giving me the strength to overcome and conquer every possible hurdle that's laid into my way.

I would like to thank Peter Collins at Polari Press for the support, patience and excitement that weaved itself through the process of publishing this collection. It was his positivity that got me so gassed up every time we spoke.

Mad love to Amy Ridler who was my ride or die editing the collection and helping on every possible end when needed.

Thank you to my dear friend Dr. Marisa Carnesky for her kind words introducing this collection, our long-lasting friendship and all the wonderful opportunities of creating performances together, to Guillermo Gomez-Peña for the radical tenderness while mentoring me and to Anne Clark for supporting my work ever since we met. Because of all your support I know I can reach the next level easy. Your love and generosity are locked into my heart forever.

Thank you to the poetry community on the Clubhouse app who welcomed me with open ears during lockdown 2020. I grew, immensely, reading my work to complete strangers during collaborative poetry sessions and creative writing sessions.

Polari Press

Taking our name from the secret slang Polari, we are an independent publishing house which seeks out hidden voices and helps them be heard.

Although Polari was spoken almost exclusively by gay and bisexual men, the nature of clandestine meetings of the mid 1900s, when homosexuality was still criminalised, brought together people from all walks of life who all had an influence on the language.

Cockney, Romany and Italian languages mixed with the colloquialisms of thespians, circus performers, wrestlers, sailors and wider criminal communities to create a slang to express their sexuality secretly and safely.

Inspired by these origins, we publish queer voices as well as other marginalised groups, to share our perspectives with each other, and help build a collaborative platform for all of us.

polari.com